... from under the bench

... from under the bench

David Best

STEELE ROBERTS
AOTEAROA NEW ZEALAND

Best, David C. (David Christopher), 1945-
From under the bench / poems by David C. Best.
ISBN 1-877338-37-0
I. Title.
NZ821.3—dc 22

Cover design: Matthew Best
Printed by Astra Print, Wellington

STEELE ROBERTS LTD
BOX 9321, WELLINGTON, AOTEAROA NEW ZEALAND
info@steeleroberts.co.nz • www.steeleroberts.co.nz

Anne

David would have loved you to have a copy

xx

If you think you will get more of God
by meditation, by devotion, by ecstasies
or by special infusion of grace
than by the fireside or in the stable —
that is nothing but taking God,
wrapping a cloak around the divine head
and shoving God under a bench.
For whoever seeks God in a special way
gets the way but misses God,
who lies hidden in it. But
whoever seeks God without any special way
gets God as God is…

from a sermon of Meister Eckhart (1260–1327)

afternoon tea

drinking softly,
sipping in the silence
through warming lips
the liquid more bitter
slightly than the lack of words
lemon-twisted

in the garden
legs stretched, ankles
crossed, cups
held saucerless
steaming in tattered wisps

no need for words
for talking
the silence couples them
zested they abandon
the world (with their shoes)

they sigh young
sighs soft as puppy barks
and sight happiness
gliding over polished grass

at wellington airport

your attention please
ladiesandgentlemmmnnn

any vehicleftunattended
ontheforecourt
willbetowedawayatt
heownersexpenseplease
collectandmove
yourunattendedvehicle
unattendedvehiclesnotmoved
willbeclamped thank you

battlelines

living in a known country
prescribed, fenced
by desperate certainty
and rootbound safe,
stockaded by a deity
who knows the rules — and
the wires — almost
as well as the troops

though god-the-giant-aspirin
is a fairy tale
the wonder stolen
and rubbed thin of laughter:
real religion is a gamble:
mystery, like unicorns, is
bothersome

9

born with great unrest,
by gift and stricture
bubbly children naughty in
discovery, still those who make
themselves afraid, trench
for us deep barricades
to snipe at what is coming
ever-becoming; they think
the mud is brighter than the sunshine

beggared

by the way he stood
it could be seen of
him he didn't trust happiness:

a man who knew his limits
even in dreams
and woke obligingly
to dawns always grey

there was no language
for his sadness
squashed deep
into alleys of the cold
grey stones
building might-haves
and wouldn't-its
he'd been too long
edged
with caution
purple like bruises
a shadow to blame
for never reaching up

beyond the waterfall

back of the Waitakeres
at the end of hidden tracks
and stubs of rainbow
Doone-like: a community
attached to the outside
by rates
and the need of supermarkets
and emails
though the water's piped muddy
by black plastic tubes
from Kawa Puka lake

a gathering like seedlings
around the main
house rooted in wrinkled grandeur,
guarded by sentinel memories
no longer at attention
(and softened now by faded colours)
and a patriarch's stubborn law:

it has no purpose
safe in the hill's dent
but the protection of the clan
and its comfort
cloistered from the wind

breathed in union with
pohutukawa gnarled with solemn age,
befriended by wildflowers
sneaking brazen into garden plots
wait for John Ridd's love
to climb
up and over the cliff

bunya

The first outline of this poem was made during a visit to the Bunya Mountains, west of Brisbane. The Bunya tree is a unique conifer which grows there (an important part of the Aboriginal diet) but it proved impossible to discover what 'Bunya' meant. It was 'just the name of the tree'. A National Park ranger told me that local tribes had recently met and agreed that its meaning was 'mother's titties'.

redefined, the tradition
has saved itself: the people
still come for nourishment —
accommodating earth and
blanketing stars given
over to adventure tenting
and mountain cabins,
chalets, lodges, air-conditioned
and cabled, the bonyi-bonyi
still nourishes

the people of the land,

those who give their
abundance away,
allow the mountain
to suckle others
who come weary to the rainforest
and its mothering breasts

the bunya nuts now
are unharvested, food
gatherers replaced by
people over-citied, worn
down by a journey different
less honest but as
meagre as any wasteland

the need for nourishment
remains, only as the
first people fitted to the land
as easily as barramundi, wallaby, snake,
we seconds own it, stand over it,
better it; we turn the dreaming
breastmilk into tourist bread

burma railway

there were ghosts
on the train
yellowing out their green youth,
dodging overcrowded heads
and hanging on
for dear death

the track clawed
along the cliff-face
desperate above the river
houseboats and party-rafts
left behind, islanded
in the sun

but the museum
was without ghosts;
there cold artefacts floated
in aching silence
deep, sharp, bright,
and tourists filed through dampened,
dumbed
by the relics

and under the bridge
for a few baht
you can ride an elephant

the ghosts understand

butterfly goodbye

something left asleep
inside me long
ago, neglected, yawned
lumbering into
change — call it a name,
touch and hold it
and let it go — moving
on... a slash of high colour
skidding through the air,
hot, jumping, silent as a glance

time to go;
and after, time not
hasty will have us
sifted, redefined,
a burying and rising,
our breath the smoke of life

comfort stop

to the left of
the bus, folks, the
town hall's
where the loos are
and again on the
left is saint pat's
built of local stone

people on the coach
wake in time to pee
and across
the road nine
country women hassle
the BVM with
light'ning devotions.

connection

for Di

wind chimes nudged by cosy
breezes slow toll, mellow
dim as if distance stretched
into marshy memory
that and in the corner
of her eyes, the purple
tinge of buddleia
with its attendant butterflies
return her to the war
as dawn parades never can

> in the disturbed soil of bombed
> streets, midden-like, the bushes were
> quickly established, weedlike,
> straggly, sham lilac on discount

the parish church bell
seeped the cruel news
of the newly dead and bomb
sites, destruction dressed,
where houses stood
and shops and schools
are vested for lent

children take shortcuts
across the scarred gaps
not knowing the butterfly plant
would be part of them now
reaching out from their past
schooling a warning across even
distant lands and new lives

this is her history, her
shaping, for it breathes and weeps,
it has escaped editors; it is connected

decoy

twin palms defy the hill
their shape so soft,
surprising, round
cut black against clouds of tin
gathering armour against thunder to come

the night sucking in its breath
a silence to reach in to
searching for secrets
listening for screams
but the silence stays
shut, intact, moving aside
for rain, thick and rowdy
like boys in a bar

the calm is ferocious, stranded…
until the rain

it comes first with the sound of crackling,
a circuit overloading
gathering voice
shouting into darkness
as if regretting the moon
till it's the only sound still alive

dialect

where do you come from?
Mosgiel
oh — snow on the ground.
she didn't mean the racing shearer's
second-cut wool,
or yet delight in
lowering of petticoats.
nothing clever
or poetic,
nothing to think over
or laugh about
over lambshank dinner

just
a cold wet word
which betrayed
a cold wet world,
snow on the ground

where there
is not laughter,
or body warmth;
where smiles hang
brulée brittle and thickened
by scorn.

drying flowers

after seeing a painting in the Western Australia Art Gallery

a gentle thing unlooked-for
against concrete rough
and chrome polished cold:
bird's-eye viewed
dots of summertime
flowers drying
       the language: imatyerre
       from utopia way (where
       else) Emily Kngwarreye
high sun colours muted
to granny greys shaded
lace fragile caught exhausted in a net of heat:
       Monet run out of paint and
       stretching the lees
her synthetic polymer paint
       moods it right
the fading flowers comment
as do shed tears rolled in dust

duet

death stood smiling,
wedding ring
on its right hand
making a hard joke
no one laughed

without ceremony it came
the dull vision of ugliness
arguing
with summer haste —
a hot wind exhausted by
distance

and sweat,
strangely chilly
death held its breath
and mine
the *contakion* breathing
comfortably

the spark inside me
unable to fight
fire with fire, dimmed
then with sudden voice
as sharp as death's probing
I began to sing
my own melody
in autumn's colours
dancing beauty

exposed

a sentinel on an altar hill
shrouded with
the mists of prayer:
    whitest bread
    encased in glass
    and gold, serenely
    and silently
    screaming
    for those who
    also have no voice

the officiant kneels low
and is blurred
in the sway of laced
smoke;
priestly tears
unseen
bespeak
outrage and impotence
    the incense rises
    mute —
    the breath
    of a significant
    conversation with God,
    the scent and smell
    of a God who
    is near

father and son

remember our row
in the starkness
of a bright winter?
— the day was as brittle
as our mood;
our words scratched
the air between us

father and son
remember how
you went off — in
fury? after
seconds all I
could manage was
shame
and a nagging
that it had gone too far

you didn't know
I spent the next
hours in panic
trying to find you
running, rushing,
darting
but I didn't know
where you'd hide
and that ignorance
haunted me
street by street

at home you
were back playing
music, too loudly

nothing was said

finn's falls

rich flesh boy
in apple glow —
a sharpness about him already
matching his autumn look
but tended
by his tender side

at six it was a smiled at
smiling thing
but he will grow to mistrust
its weakness
before it settles gentle on him
and he allows it air

for now Phineas plunders life
for fiction
playing by his stream trickle-tumbling
down the bank
somersaulting from earth
dense as mudcake

made by his aunt, she
calls it Finn's Waterfall

the splash is dancing diamonds
coloured half-life
between day and night
and its music-magic — a laughter
pitched so high not even farm dogs
can hear, but only boys —
will call him back,
root him in this
thick chocolaty dirt

food chain

the tardy notice said
to prevent forest fire
but the loggers

prevented first
the land was latticed
spelked so badly

even the mist's
hollow cough
comes too late
brittled and snapped

sharp with flint-edged angles
the land is indifferent
to torture and torturers
soon it will give
suck to little trees

young trees
aspiring trees breathing
in its muck
to be turned
into our greenless future
and when the wind would play
instead it slides
moaning
over forest stubble
bluntly shaved
and cut

oh had they left
the trees to wild green gracious
in blessing
to the champagne mist
to our carefulness and
the tui's song
to taste the breath of clouds
and hongi with the sun

for critics of spong

stuff
it into a bag
and put it
under the bench

god's head
in plain brown paper
safe as may be

stop the wind
at jerningham point
bouncing off
gateways
tugging
at the roof of the church;
insist the sun
fizzle
dribbling yolk
behind the rimutaka
ranges

glory

muffled timpani of rain
trickled into warm waking,
after

by the bed
blinds slatted ceiling to floor
harped by the night breeze fingering
a maccabaeus flutter;
you lie deep
in rainshine shade

muted victory
smiling back to sleep,
after

graveside

sad faces
standing still
untouched even
by music that would make
them whole again

the music
of voices gentle
with impotence
the music
of tears stolen
from wounded eloquence
the music
of silence
misted, frosted
by impatience

still faces
standing sad
gripped in agonies
unknown
untouchable
as in the first experience
of death

standing faces
sad still
resolute
and the music is the
thud of clay in
the rain

they'll bring in
a digger later
and the music
will be too loud to bear

growing pains

his face
too bright for nature
reaches out its warmth,
winning friends

he already knows
the perils of routine
so crashes into his world
with unthought carefulness
and his eyes
grow used with knowledge

innocence and appetite
like splashes of colour
that capture divinity
are his seductive treasure
and his undoing

harbour crossing

after the rains
hazelnut water escaped
their valleys
and turned the Hokianga
thin caramel

low hills lay
prone across the water,
feminine,
all arms and legs and
rounded breasts
naked except
for the fine down
of dust-coloured grass

Kohu Ra Tuarua
white-gleamed and whining
pressed eighteen vehicles
on board
for the pull from Kohukohu
to Rawene
and people cramped inside
fog the glass
waiting for flame trees
on the other side to warn
and warm our way
to Auckland

home
coming

with a truffle
fork I
could trace dead
leaves and debris
from broom honey myrtle
and unearth
rhizanthella gardneri, babakin
orchids for short

but cream
cakes and milo
at the women's institute
hall, a fund raiser,
will have to do
truffle forks are
hard to come by

we head home into
a single malt glow
a safe-in-the-arms
of Jesus sunset

honeygatherer

no final word of
wisdom
in death, not
a goodbye even,
just the life
now set and settled
and beyond sting

there
was
a life of wisdom,
blue-bruised, scared,
made sacred with
smiles
and the honeysweetness
of love

her body had given
us life; hers was the voice which
called us together:
in her foundations
dug deep,
the friendship
and hope of history,
the buzz
of family, and now
dead there was
boxed-in silence

      that final gift:
      her silence paraded
      the freedom she always
      offered
      which had, by
      whatever amount we'd
      accepted,
      shaped what she had made

hotel

a room with space but
without conversation, memory
loss and in need of paint
and hammer and curtains
other than worn mauve ruffled

the mirror doors
hold in their
sight nothing of the
bed, so secrets
and entertainment are
scarce, empty
and archbishop jenson
knitting in his palace
will be pleased

it's good for
fitful sleeping only,
traffic noise stamped on the night,
the drum of rain, the
rush of wind,
bellow of drunks

it would be dilatory
to die in this room
even in bed

in my arms

the future walking
short-stepped, fitful,
gushed... stumbling becomes
the future carried
smooched without care
or thought of snot,
worrying into my neck

not even wondering when
the milk will next appear
or how: trust on legs too
short, but with arms
vicelike and guts
which ponder the
centrality of things
and have tested
the rightsideup of what matters

in search of a poem

need-to-know words
clatter for space in the
Herald
headlines, made of
edges 36pt sharp
and noisy as chainsaws
clipped words
cruel in brevity, plain
compressed
in column centimetres
yapping the world's
nonsense

while all that was
necessary:
a smile memories
are repaired by
a melody of words to sing by —
jigsaw words
round-edged
safe for children

just kidding

with jeans' crutch
sunk around the knees
and a sullen look,
with cares and woes
and attitude

hey you, boy; yes
you, what
you got to be
so disdainful about?

eh? the sun shines
you go home via
KFC and you don't
even have spots

juxtaposition

puffed, mildly,
in my soft middle age
by the gentle
hill-work walk
through Rotoiti beeches

once
wonderingly remembered
it was the puffiness
of smooth-faced years
eager in a softness
downed by
sharp Scafell winds

> youth walking for
> granted
> in ancient hills
> which promised the silence
> of secrets

and now in age
closed by ripe woods
tall bluenight
mountains spill down
the secrets of silence

hushed in the beard of bush
I am newly birthed
and wet with love

from arid moor
to yearning forest

kid with a hankering

horse's necks
more bubbles than brandy
in the
king's head
years before it
became a retirement
home,
and a pipe
of no consequence
— just two bob and
some coppers —

not a success
even after the
coughing stopped and
it was easier
keeping stoked

the yellow stem
imitating ivory
clashed against teeth
a commentary spoiled

pinched an old one of my
dad's, dusty on
the mantle, mellowed
crusty, vile

charles dickens stayed
in the king's
working on *nicholas nickleby*.
I wonder
if he had a pipe
stalking the moors
looking for Spike

kings cross girl

sleep deprived not
sleepy, a scant
girl, the finest
six-thirty in the morning
girl in the cross

not saying much
stands sloven
hipped, knee bent,
out front the burger
bar weighing up the
young drunks going home
at last, stumbled, glassy,
heavy, offering
them company or anything
you want

the sign in the window
says *take aways*

labour day
at paraparaumu beach

tonsured sky frost-thin
fringed in eggshellblue
trapping a white sun

the first settled
heat of spring
presided over by
a moody Kapiti
brooding in greened
dark mystery
cool as breathing shadows
a salad of air and light

celebrating a long engagement
with the past

in bad weather
or in air dulled
by lesser expectations
of winter clarity
the island will growl
menace in the water:

> distant shouts of
> warriors skim offshore
> and blood spill
> will taint the sunset
> craving revenge…
> listen…

the crack of the tokotoko
melds with
the clack of irons
on Paraparaumu golf course

landscape

our hills are not
silent but
shout tall
our rivers sing
their own
song to southern seas
our birds have
no foreign language
our light has
its own brightness
our night
the black of homely black
our sun warms
our wind cleans
bodies which are colded here
and splendidly selfsoiled
our sweat waters the earth
and gives hearty growth,
filling our geography
with the art and dreams
which spill
from our being
and shapes our clay.

when will we learn
that imported wisdom
is a landscape
of little joy?

language difficulties

captain cook would
still know whitby,
thin and greyish, ripe
for escape, a spit
of a harbour,
but sydney would take
his breath by surprise

in hyde park he stands
bronzed waving
and on his lips almost
a "now then, lads"
rallying his crew together

his back is
to a skyscraper
sporting huge amex
signage squinting
down on australia's
glorious dead:
push with george
dubya bush
different dialects

now then, lads

leaving

goodbyes aren't thought
in advance but suddenly
stun, like loud music,
regret and relief jostling
us between

out of breath senses
donate an awkwardness
ghosted by every separation
significant and shaping,
wadded now by the
rush to be gone,
selfhood making shy excuse

here's to a pleased
new year

lilac in George Street

passed in the street
the city no longer at home,
resting less easy
the familiar made grey-distant
at once lilac, drugging the air
    tugs the distance
    the George Street stroll stopped
    dead in its tracks
lilac! at once there's shallow sun
    of early spring
    and grassed smells
    thundering trucks robbed of their stink

    the noise even of unhappiness
    not strong enough to dominate, but
    dampened by Advent purple
    and Easter white mingled scents
    promises
    which gather behind the eyes
    and linger

lilac to live by
    rescuing something good
    that was lost or forgotten
    or tamped down,
and be gladder at what is

litany

from things
uncomfortable which
don't sit well

from blistering tongues
as pink
as sunburn

from feckless
fortune, chance

jigsaw-puzzled pain

deliver us not
good Lord.

look out

it will be a day of summer, sunblotched
and sweaty, as if the two hundred
million dollar flood had never been,
or is as a dream
remembered badly
except for the path through the bush
to the lookout

disguised, shrouded by
palms snapped, death
brown, smelly now in the
quick heat, shaken to
the forest floor by winds
mindless of direction once
they'd bounced off kapiti,
and scoured by rain heartless
and heaving, churning
the path to deceit

the sun plays with it now, dancing
too late but to court all
decay and smile patient, playful
but seriously waiting...

you won't make the lookout —
for now step warily, the
way isn't easy to find

looking ahead

not ours
the future has to
be glorious —
though settle for
better — if
not in itself then
in its memory

it's the lasting
trick of middle age
whose july eyes
squinted against the
cold, squash up
to hope
on first name basis

the perjury
risen in descant
is quickly taken in mistake
for melody

but
there's always
heaven

low hanging fruit

dangerous conversations
make me easy
picking,
dribbling ripe
bruise ready

dangerous conversations
nursing
sickly weaknesses
which leave me
limp, sweaty

dangerous conversations
full of grey-hot hope,
looking for
trim triumph
smartly turned out,
bright as daisies

don't
speak to me in
whispered confidence
in your summer voice
hazed as sulphur

don't expect
me to be more than I am,
but doubt
my lusciousness
and leave me to the sun

martyr's complex

my passion is for the impossible
— that the cancer grow green
— that the storm bring only warmth and glow
— that the world will see beyond itself
  and so become itself

for the autumn leaf
  flame and gold
  will stay ever live on its tree

but love frightens
— it is surrender
  a mothering of Christ
  an invitation
for suffering to come and get me

melody

chimes nudged to tune
by the accidental
brush
of the shoulder
of the wind
— a tune in freefall
but more fitting
than the voices
in the background
I hear
making plans
and organising the music
of others,
crackling

echoing mellow
the chimes call
us to hold
with our setting, where
all nurture is
— but we, strident, would
rather take control
and blame the consequences
on some fickle god

milkweed

parachuting dock
clocks
silver swirling
whirling to the ground,
hope breezed, rippling
like teased
water, tail-feather
fronds darting
minnows in green
shallows
rarely seen

and now to lie in patience
unlikely to strike
gold there,
though it's possible

fall at random
die barren
yet come the summer
there will be
monarch butterflies feeding
nothing more sure,
and swans laying
more seeds
with einstein hair

motto

the council rubbish
dump
with its stink like the breath
of hell is our field
of dreams —
terror and tears
turned not for fantasy
but to purpose

if you search
for treasure there
squelching in the muck,
hoping

remember me

it's not a bad prayer:
chance to have
your pinned heart
touched not in pity
or even sympathy

remember me

and the air stirs
hot breathed fetid

at the tip
it will be enough

new age

a slow dull day
like those before
and those still feared,
life to be hobbled through
the mind
limping, the heart arched
with aching
because God is dead
succumbed to grey duty
and sad mistake
that's how it was before the war
    but life
    now is snatched
    at and saints, not prayed to, are
    alive — they play rugby and golf and
    have bodyguards. God
    is a cricketer with
    a place in the record books
modern theology:
two wrongs make a right

newsunday

secret people
spilt by the sun
and bent on indulgence
wandering languid
sighing into filtered shadows
the glide of warm
apple juice surfing the
breeze, high-hearted

dazzling people dazzled
by the slowness
of the day, parading
as in a mime
their secrets on show
but safe, unexplained
a rushpush of people
couples showing each other off,
small crowds gaudy as parrots
loners enjoying disconnected
company, children raw with
tiredness, gasped
olds sucking on hot colours
deliberate, aching
for a cuppa and a gossip

and in the men's now
there are full facilities
for babies to be changed
and a queue

partita for one voice

it used to be
safe
and respected
it used
to bring the relief
you get
when you've crept
out of a hospital
room
and the watching
is not a burden

but now
when
someone tells me
I know what I believe
eyes down
I fend them off
with *Yes*
that's what scares
me.

regular maintenance

combed,
explored
by isopropyl alcohol
optimally conditioned,
ice-smarted clean,
soft-cleaned: humming
and receptive
my son in London
faxed a few
words and
a picture
of himself as tourist
but I forget exactly
where
except there were
pigeons

an electronic embrace
only slightly
loosened by
the ether of
distance

rehearsal

on their hot wet brows
winter is unlocked, chilled on
the hill —
a throwing off place
rock-bare of reason
and convenient for low fear,
their spirits, minds in flush
and their bodies obeying,
lungs and larynxes conspired
for peace
blood

hustle him up the trail;
trial run...

grim delight does the shoving
familiar contempt for the
familiar: frogmarched up
the hill —
anger walling a worried space,
winding people together
in a shroud of dissatisfaction

this'll teach you to know
your place...

what did they expect?
a wimpish God isn't enough?

throw him over, off
the hill...

not yet:
he slips through the
crowd, not leaving
them at all.

reliquary

the safeness we forced
on God has diluted
and remembered daisychain
summers
are no buffer

those a-drowse with fear
take god-the-giant-aspirin
once a week
and say the pain
has gone away

religion walks with a limp—
the love it swanks
neglected, dragging slow

their book promises
life lavished
but they scuttle into
its pages and
stand with flimsy effort
hands on hips

retraining

we are afraid of
silence,
so darkness is
no more
than the absence
of light,
and the meaning of our dance
is masked in spent movement

so has it never been
all right to fail

because we are
guardians of a collective
story
a brave face is essential
soaped well
and massaged pink-fresh
in water harsh
with purity

we believe in
death after life

reveille

quietly just before the sun appears
the wahlenbergia sighs awake
tinkling in the dawn,
and devil's guts twist, almost
soundless, but managing a
stretching rustle
noisy friarbirds shudder and ruffle
and soon duet with blue-faced
honeyeaters,
their yakka climbing,
clamouring, roused by
light and budding warmth

the kak-kak-kak
dollarbird solos clear against
the chattering, and the warbling
of the fairy-wren flits scraps of red
flutter, flap
into the forming morning music

as pelicans yawn their clacks
the sea's percussion is
somehow more regulated
now, lapping
the land in time; whales blow hissing spray
as the sun is greeted
and whirling beyond all is the morepork's
seeping chorus,
wrapped in the wind exhaling

even the waking newcomers
are accommodated: distant
hammers eat each other's
echo; mechanical diggers clang, drag;

buzzsaws struggle for their note
punctuated by the low
resonance of ants' dull march
in their millions;
the percussion of vehicles swishing,
tearing the air,
dogbark syncopation,
crunch of toast, ring of teaspoon,
cry of baby unbreasted

riverwalk

hibiscus purpled
plucked from a
pulsating
rainbow so
bright it hurts the eyes
startles the senses,
and hung on
silver steel colonnades
like tusks
winding a walk by the river

the steel is cunning:
masked as support
it is the parasite
of the flowers
fragile and brittle
like tissue shallow
fried in violet
ink, brittle

naughty dreamtime
crows strut black
scoffing
and all the
fountains which
would water paradise
smell of chlorine

shadow of wings

it feels like something
great's going to
happen, something too
big to sneak past,
something beautifully
another...
an idea's birth?
a coming to terms?
hand holding hand,
perhaps;
it's hidden from me
though I know it's cornflower
blue and sharp as
ecstasy, creamy with
pain

it stalks me
friendly, but its time
will come.

signpost

not as final as a
grave...
scarecrow, more;
a cross on the fence
badly fixed
with wire,
painted gritty white
and hissed at in derision

the embarrassed
plastic flowers which bloom there
have it right:
practical icons, drained of colour
and draining a blessing from
whispering tears.

no birds sing
because life is warned off.

64

slayer of dragons

a boy from
wellington wrote to
me saying it was
good I was there as
he searched for
god,
all smiles
his letter
and frothed with
confidence

how would it have
been if I'd helped him
find his car keys in
the rush of a
morning?
ironed his shirt and,
ah,
so sweetly kissed
him
so he would go
out nicely
to save the world?

stand-off

the rhythm
of half wisdom rails
and twists:
arms me for
fight
against the blackness
of night —
though black is its nature
and a potential friend

no one told me
growing old is
ordinary,
the settling of experience

but here is newness
at which to take fright
perhaps,
but we come to age equipped;
it's adorned with our growth

as you go
up the steps
sensibly hold onto the rails

street

no one ever
walks the street
— it goes
nowhere except to
homes partitioned
off by sentinel gum trees
and scrub

shops? no
no pub or church
or community hall,
neighbours so far
apart in
separate fiefdoms
without names or open doors

bees, butterflies,
birds keep them
in touch, bear the
gossip,
along with the low
low echo of
dogs talking with each
other across fencelines
and gullies

but no-one on the footpath
no child with trike
no sales pitch
no Mormons

sunday morning boys

sun's in
and the lads are out,
jeans' hip sagging
(and the hips too lean
to saunter and roll,
they baggily slouch, sexless)
wandering in car yards
wistfully
wishfully
stroking
sleep-red paintwork

some, a few,
alone, some
small-grouped,
with sons along
to share safe bonding
prescribed by neutral
icons manly as
football boots

it's even okay to push
still-milk babies,
gather them, sleeping,
to the shade of a twin-cam
saloon,
a screaming sedan

solo dads
doing sunday duty,
cuddling up to what
might have been

tailfeathers

not the years of acceleration yet
these swampy years are
slow
at memory making

slow as sleep
they'll gather speed come their time:
winds gathering leaves
rustling them to their
end
soon, soon enough, too soon

much quicker are older years
still
with time to dawdle over all that was,
real, imagined; cataloguing
from studied distances,
slight
and far away

guiding, making flightpaths
in the sequences,
making
sure they weren't just
random

taonga

deep under ferns
a tweed stream veins
the land,
water stroking
rock green as moss,
lifed liquid
rock, treasured:
the greenstone treasure
of a people,
calling them to worth

> death turned love
> green by traditions and
> understandings,
> a force strong
> as motherhood

greening
in death

flowing on

tasting

swirled flash
of oiled green
be quick to spot
melon-orange sheen
delicate as sunlit dust
glance quick off the rim

      look
      linger

oak-heavy
a dryness catching
the back of the throat,
overtaken by
marmalade which has
taken its jacket off
to dance with clean
white peaches

      inhale
      imagine

earth and leather
blunting sweet-edgedness
to purple plums
rich and royal

      sip
      savour

spit
rinse

territory

chaffinch in on
the Wellington breeze
your
bowing flight interrupted
you perch daintily
prideful
on advent — grey pohutakawa
promising for Christmas and
sing your declamatory carol

voiced sharp and harpy
at odds with your
chested red slightness
you declare
boundaries with belligerence

so
do I — we cannot help it

the church entails
my song but
as the wind dilutes yours

the
bright strand
between

noise was shattered
by silence
silver-framed and
shifting,
stroked by yellow
breezes   *tui, tui, tuituia*

the top   *tuia i runga*
and bottom bound   *tuia i raro*
together by the
light

the pink   *tuia i roto, tuia i waho*
greyblue lies gentle
of the vital day   **73**
between the waking
sky and
stirring earth
like the promise
of kisses
the impulse
of life stirs
nativity red
soldered by sunshafts

far horizons smile
the ruffling clay
sprouting
unfolding and brazen I
stretch
and push
tying the music
of creation
to my belt

                    ka tika

the chalice

cupped by the
blackness,
the guardian of creation
cradles my
body

and spills
me
to open up the dark

I taste the
breath
of all that is
and am written
straight
where
just a moment ago there
was brokenness

poured deep,
soaking into the blood
of the land
I am offered
not for greed
not in fancy

I am offered
for happiness:
angel of annunciation

ah so beautiful
is the still hour
of the sea's withdrawal,
rhymed
with the breathing
sea's return

pressing on,
urgent in life

the singer

genius in its own
space
retreating, retreating
eyes down
captured by the song
exploding
leaping black
daring

God listens proud
and withdraws —
now there's
room
for your magnificat

this way

roads are in
tiers fetchingly,
arching, bending
in imitation
of the river's
ebbing,
concrete gangplanks

they curl at last
inwards and sweep
unseen humming into
gothic-ish chasms of the city
to become enmeshed,
gridded

the river
wanders full
slow,
embracing its own
dissipation,
to the sea

totems

mother of life, a word,
an aside
as we smile on
your gifts of colours
and shapes
with eyes
skinned for
the looking
and with hearts
cupped for receiving,
a word, an apology:

sacred and inviolate
are the creatures
of our totems;
thus have you conserved
the life of the land

often there is the question
of why the people
are not totems too,
then black and white
caught
up in thriving respect
would learn to live
together

but your rainbow colours are
dulled as
they're mined and dug
or set in necklaces
and the totems
are stolen for the new
religion
where now the crow's people?
where the kangaroo?

hear of the magpies,
the soaring hawks,
the black brother swans?

not in rainbow colours,
but more tawdry;
not in the silence
of the people's traditions,
or restrained movement
which shows respect
aaaaeeee
the colour and shape of things
has lesser meaning
this is a stealing
like many others
which is regretted,
mother of life
this is what I say

training tree

the nuns knew about shaping
shapeless in long black
knees calloused
by bare flagstones
prayed hollow long before them.

> *a small kettle*
> *holed by the boiling*
> *and hung heavy on a noose of string*

faces rosy and taught by the
concentration of late and early prayer
attuned to catch every nuance of the divine voice

> *string and half a brick from the garden*
> *dangling, bobbing, pulling*

feet flat from the walking to teach sad children;
and hands red from vegetable water
scrubbing and scalding
smiles haunted by kindness

> *worn pieces of cutlery and halves of scissors*
> *wrapped in cellotape to mute the metal*
> *swinging on string and*
> *stretching green wood.*

the tree will at last be draped and eloquent
won into improvement.

verismo

the too hearty
noise of the
world
fails to
see its limits even
in dream
raking over
the reasons for its pain

it huddles
shoulders crunched
against the nice
wind and
bright moon,
and barges on
frowned with fatigue

while notes green
with life
shoots of sound not
to rescue
but to reform
yawn gently
protecting the shade
of their shapes
like a man who's been
a long time
alone I'm
unbuttoned,
shared pain fused,
by the music

visiting

twice foreign I come,
double white,
fearful that my step
will be one
too many for this
vigorous land turned
fragile
     — not fragile of life
     but of humanity
     not fragile of spirit
     but of substance
     not fragile of smile
     but in fear
     of a brief history
     which tortures antiquity

listen though
hotchpotch of blood pumps
my heart, and now
Aotearoa has tutored me
and it's easy to see
my faded brownness,
the result only
of cold easterlies and snow
and sun shyness,
can be loved
for what I am

as I come to your place
with my stepping
I lay down a koha:
     my *alcheringa*
     is being expanded, new-dimensional
     — an exciting time
     for both of us
stoop and pick it up; it is of the heart

---

*alcheringa: Aboriginal word for the 'Dreamtime' —
the creation of the universe*

wairarapa gardens

smoky hot rocks
the colour of bright
pumice grey the lawn's
green so it looks
high summer worn
and sweetpeas
smell pastel good

a ginko tree guardian
of nature's wisdom fans
and flaps in the movement
of air as magnolia ivory
rusts, gentility fallen
on hard times

old roses graceful
tease the glowing afternoon
with venerable scents for
which even the goldfish
remember no words in their lazy
round of feeding, glinting
sliding into slimed shadows

it's too hot for tennis
too tranquil for croquet
painlessly slow for cricket
over-hushed for chess

dragonflies sleep on dried
old sleepers and the worms are
silent

waiting game

dingy, looking dead,
pretending,
against the strident
blue sky searching
to siphon the breath of
leaves,
bruised gums silently
thin, dusted blue grey
with pink patches, slight
as a blush,
like sunburn under the skin

wait for the
rain,
teased by distant
puffs of cloud

the sky plays
its relentless game
and the earth soft-pants
its dusty obligation

but sometime
the gums will lend
us their breath again
and creation will
unclench

walk in the park

the wet-earthed garden
ruffled by rumours
as the wind
stirs history
and blood

the kiss
of the night
tear-drained, ashen black;
the wind
stirs history
and strains on wood

fumbled confusion over there
trodden scared
by the soldier discipline
of lesser men
as the wind
stirs history
and dances to the rhythm of hate

the hour is late;
liturgies and candles are doused —
their memory echo-curls and dissipates

it's time for trial,
and home
as the wind with meadow-green voice
stirs history
and lies in wait.

walking away

the sound of my walking
precise as fingerprints
even in shoes not new

tart on floorboards,
satisfying noise;
the thinness of leather
on pavement
crisp, snappy;
scraping warm gravel
with buttery smell

you love the sound
of your feet, boy;
her voice limiting
cold as iron fencing,
stepping
sounds are suspect
more than they should be;
walk quietly...

as if you didn't exist walk
soundless
you have nowhere to go

weather forecast

grimaced wind
whooshing from every direction
in drunken dance
whistling urgently
without tune
the earth itself writhed
and thrashing
birthing and fighting
    new life is too difficult
and exhausting
(the dawn is hours away yet)

tree limbs turned
into lashes
with flaying leather tips, slashing
what happened
what happened to gentle?
winter does not die well,
and spring?
well, spring won't let go
now it's tasted
the old season's fear

it's a fight to the death
so the wind
spends itself in furious bursts

it will all be over
by morning

wednesday sun

life away from here
can only be guessed at, so
brittle,
black clouds nudging moonlight
edges, muted
     ah, here comes the day
     certain bright:
     experience and potential
     coupled
yes, go
burn a slow orange disappearance

wellington

michaelmas daisies on kaiwharawhara
gorges shine
like granite dusted with rain,
silver-purple sharp

clouds arching down
the city is lost in bright
rain and light:
a shekinah
delivering labour-day travellers
safe to the harbour,
the day closed in,
caped and hooded
mysterious as fog
the colour of egg yolks and sugar

hillside roads gleaming and steaming
the air shifting cold
in pockets where the wind is torn
pushing smells of shallow sea
and deep-frying grease along
oriental parade

old men holding down their hats
walk, leaning, for their health